YOUNG
TEDDY ROOSEVELT

Written and illustrated by Cheryl Harness

NATIONAL
GEOGRAPHIC
SOCIETY

Washington D.C.

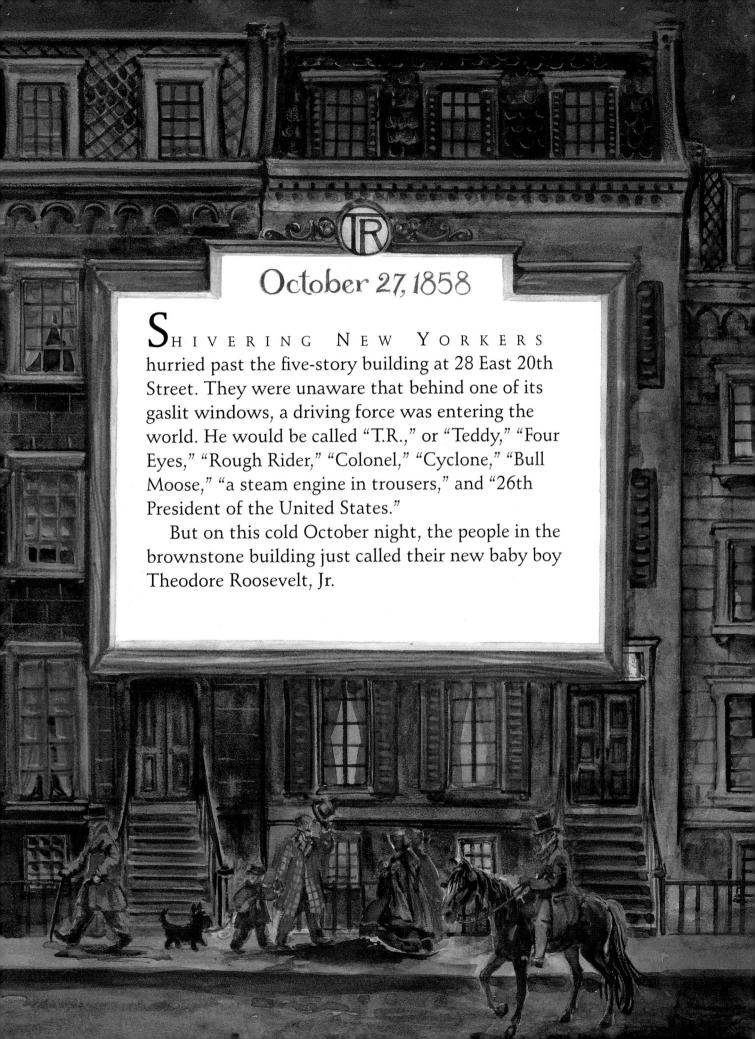

October 27, 1858

SHIVERING NEW YORKERS hurried past the five-story building at 28 East 20th Street. They were unaware that behind one of its gaslit windows, a driving force was entering the world. He would be called "T.R.," or "Teddy," "Four Eyes," "Rough Rider," "Colonel," "Cyclone," "Bull Moose," "a steam engine in trousers," and "26th President of the United States."

But on this cold October night, the people in the brownstone building just called their new baby boy Theodore Roosevelt, Jr.

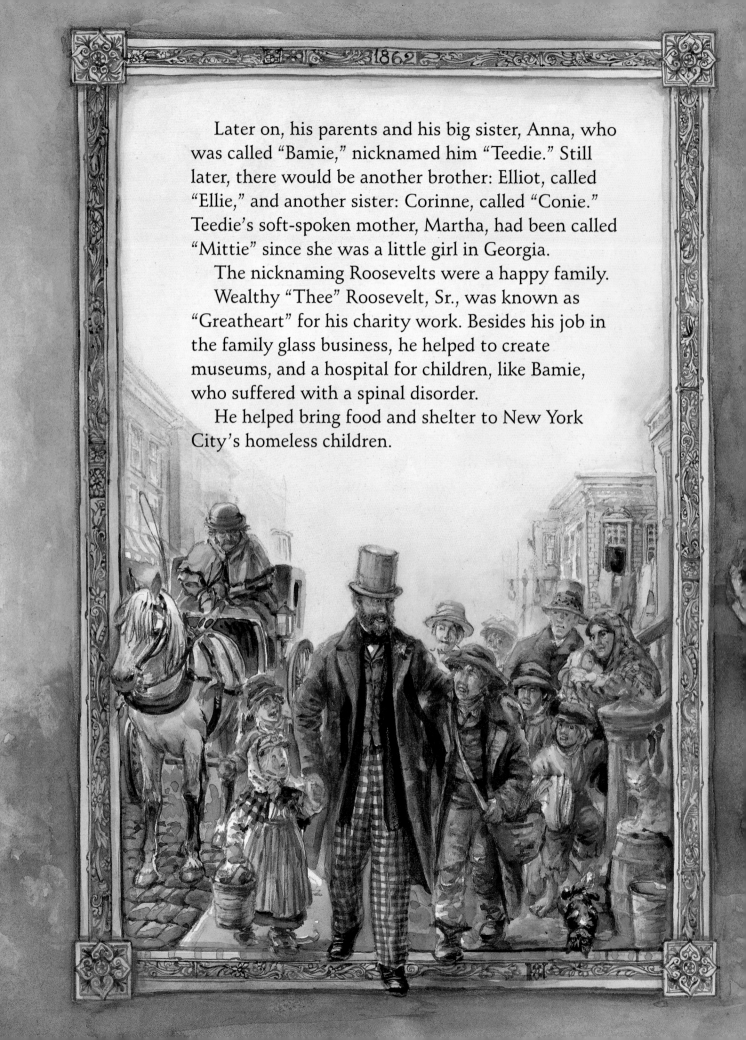

Later on, his parents and his big sister, Anna, who was called "Bamie," nicknamed him "Teedie." Still later, there would be another brother: Elliot, called "Ellie," and another sister: Corinne, called "Conie." Teedie's soft-spoken mother, Martha, had been called "Mittie" since she was a little girl in Georgia.

The nicknaming Roosevelts were a happy family.

Wealthy "Thee" Roosevelt, Sr., was known as "Greatheart" for his charity work. Besides his job in the family glass business, he helped to create museums, and a hospital for children, like Bamie, who suffered with a spinal disorder.

He helped bring food and shelter to New York City's homeless children.

ROOSEVELTS

In 1861, three-year-old Teedie's country and his parents were divided. Mama's heart was torn between her Northern Yankee husband and her Rebel brothers, who were fighting for the South. Thee was for President Lincoln and believed in the Union, but rather than hurt his wife and her family, he regretfully did what many rich men did then. He paid a poor man to go to war in his place.

Some days, when Father was away on business, Teedie and Bamie helped Mama fill boxes with clothing and medicine to be mysteriously smuggled past the blockade of Union gun ships into Mama's home-land: enemy territory. It was like a game, Teedie thought. He loved to wear his Union uniform and play "running the blockade" with Bamie, the Rebel.

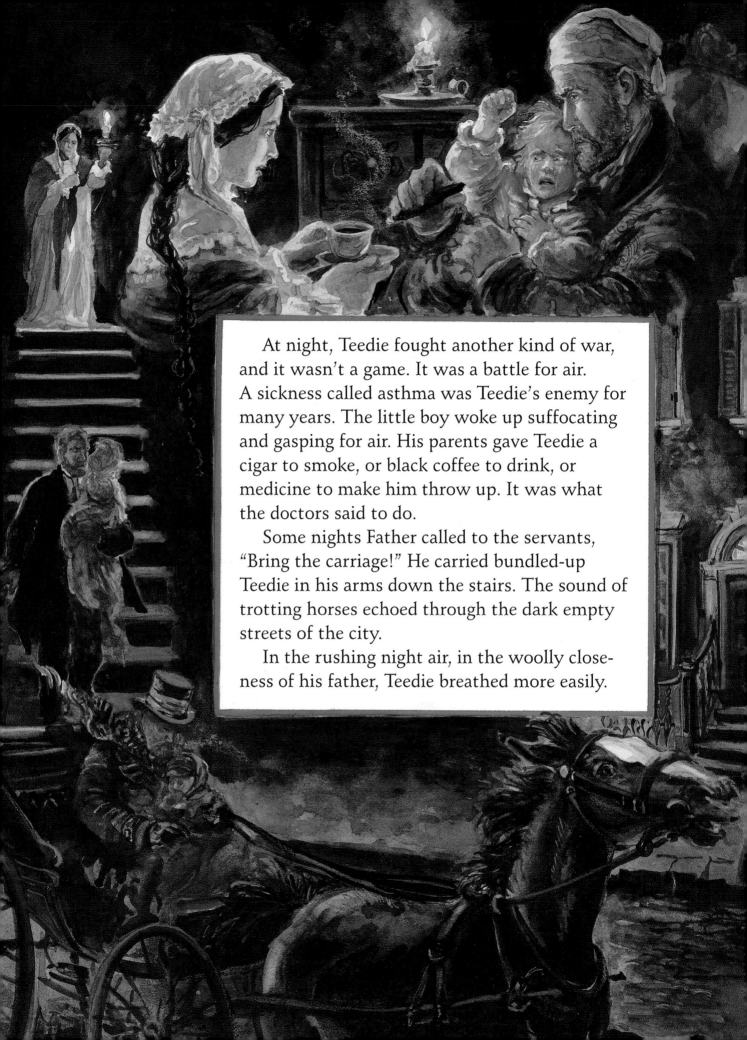

At night, Teedie fought another kind of war, and it wasn't a game. It was a battle for air. A sickness called asthma was Teedie's enemy for many years. The little boy woke up suffocating and gasping for air. His parents gave Teedie a cigar to smoke, or black coffee to drink, or medicine to make him throw up. It was what the doctors said to do.

Some nights Father called to the servants, "Bring the carriage!" He carried bundled-up Teedie in his arms down the stairs. The sound of trotting horses echoed through the dark empty streets of the city.

In the rushing night air, in the woolly close-ness of his father, Teedie breathed more easily.

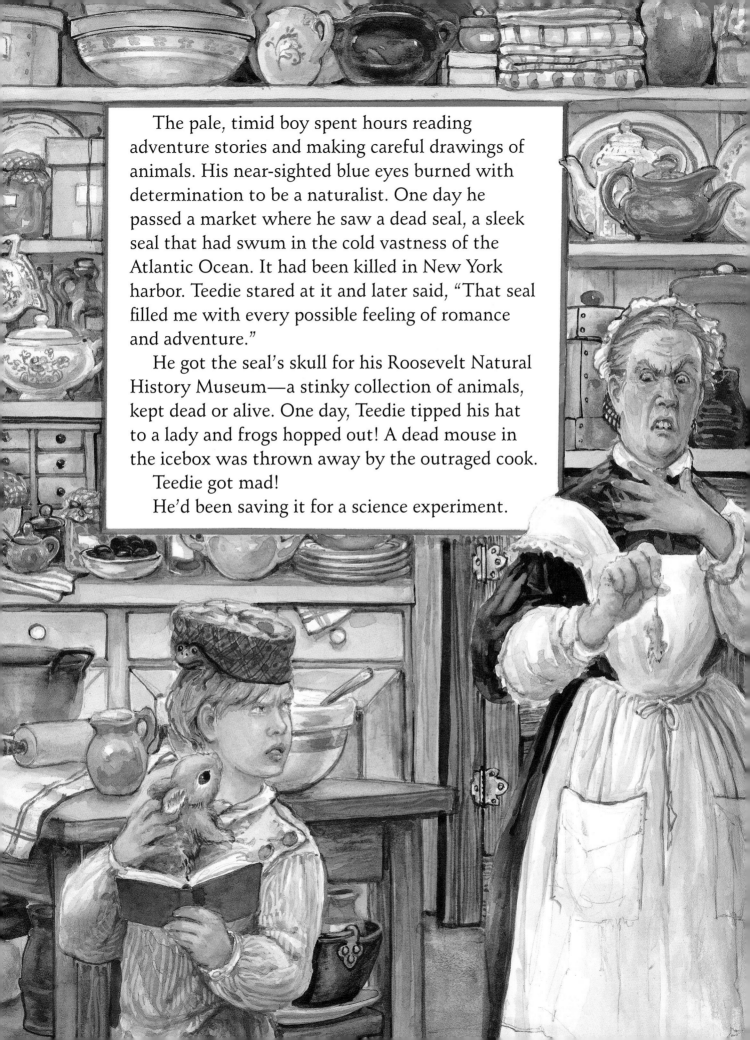

The pale, timid boy spent hours reading adventure stories and making careful drawings of animals. His near-sighted blue eyes burned with determination to be a naturalist. One day he passed a market where he saw a dead seal, a sleek seal that had swum in the cold vastness of the Atlantic Ocean. It had been killed in New York harbor. Teedie stared at it and later said, "That seal filled me with every possible feeling of romance and adventure."

He got the seal's skull for his Roosevelt Natural History Museum—a stinky collection of animals, kept dead or alive. One day, Teedie tipped his hat to a lady and frogs hopped out! A dead mouse in the icebox was thrown away by the outraged cook.

Teedie got mad!

He'd been saving it for a science experiment.

Father and Mother decided that a tour of Europe would be educational for their children and the change might be healthy for puny Teedie. So they went on board the *Scotia,* the fastest paddle steamer to Europe.

Bamie stayed behind at a boarding school near Paris.

The Roosevelt family returned home a year later, on May 25, 1870. Teedie wrote in his diary, "New York!!! Hip! Hurrah! What a bustle we had getting off."

Roosevelt Grand Tour 1869-1870

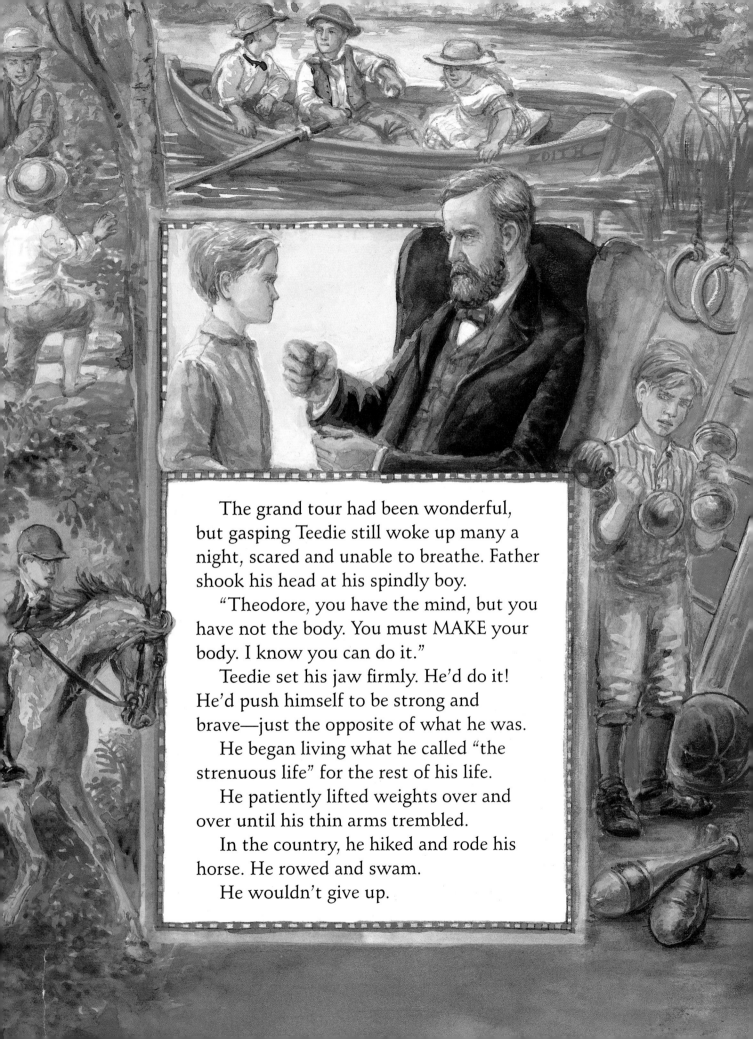

The grand tour had been wonderful, but gasping Teedie still woke up many a night, scared and unable to breathe. Father shook his head at his spindly boy.

"Theodore, you have the mind, but you have not the body. You must MAKE your body. I know you can do it."

Teedie set his jaw firmly. He'd do it! He'd push himself to be strong and brave—just the opposite of what he was.

He began living what he called "the strenuous life" for the rest of his life.

He patiently lifted weights over and over until his thin arms trembled.

In the country, he hiked and rode his horse. He rowed and swam.

He wouldn't give up.

By the time his family traveled again, bespectacled Teedie still had asthma and other problems, but he was a stronger boy who tramped along the river under the Egyptian sun. He hunted birds so he could study and stuff them for his museum. The blasting of his shotgun boomed across the Nile. When he returned to the family's rented houseboat—called a *dahabeah*—Mittie laughed as she whisked back her white skirts.

"Teedie, look at your muddy self!"

Day after day, Papa and Bamie stared as he pulled dead herons, egrets, larks, pelicans, and doves out of his bag. Everyone watched as he carefully skinned and stuffed the birds. Conie held her nose. "Eeuww, Teedie!" He smelled like taxidermy chemicals and bird guts. Ellie cried, "Listen to my poem!" It began:

There was an old fellow named Teedie
Whose clothes at best looked so seedy....
Teedie's grin shone white in his muddy face.

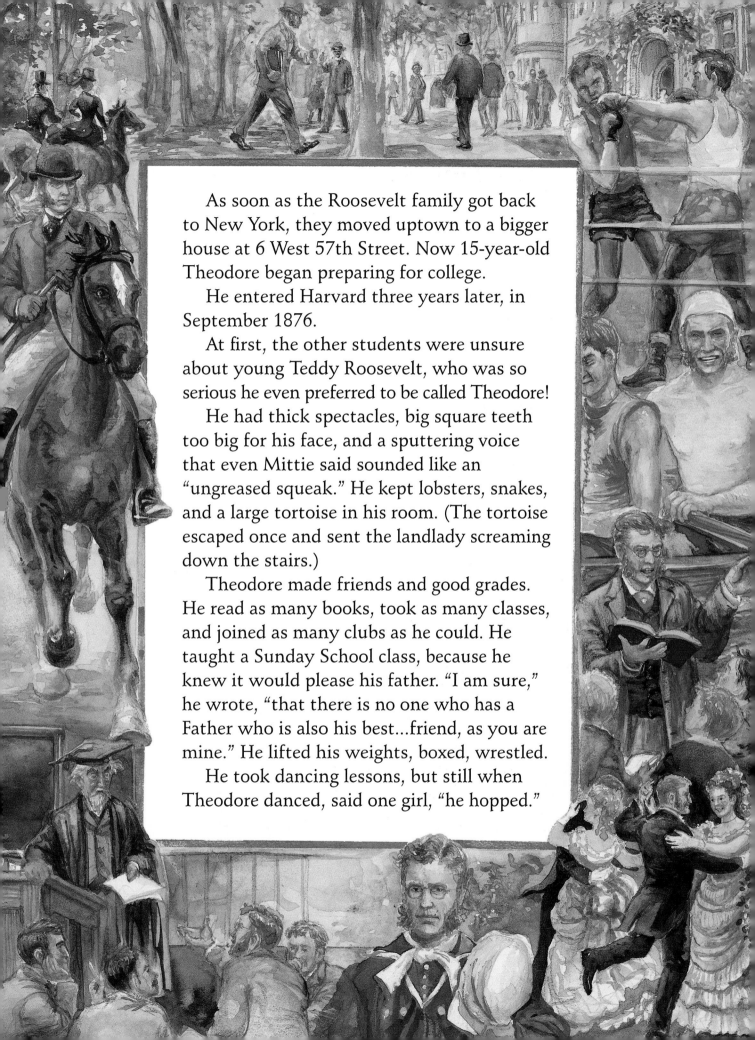

As soon as the Roosevelt family got back to New York, they moved uptown to a bigger house at 6 West 57th Street. Now 15-year-old Theodore began preparing for college.

He entered Harvard three years later, in September 1876.

At first, the other students were unsure about young Teddy Roosevelt, who was so serious he even preferred to be called Theodore!

He had thick spectacles, big square teeth too big for his face, and a sputtering voice that even Mittie said sounded like an "ungreased squeak." He kept lobsters, snakes, and a large tortoise in his room. (The tortoise escaped once and sent the landlady screaming down the stairs.)

Theodore made friends and good grades. He read as many books, took as many classes, and joined as many clubs as he could. He taught a Sunday School class, because he knew it would please his father. "I am sure," he wrote, "that there is no one who has a Father who is also his best...friend, as you are mine." He lifted his weights, boxed, wrestled.

He took dancing lessons, but still when Theodore danced, said one girl, "he hopped."

On February 10, 1878, Theodore pushed through the crowd of people, including many sad and ragged children who had been helped by his father.

He dashed up the stairs, his overcoat billowing, a crumpled telegram in his pocket, but he was too late. His father had died, of cancer, the night before.

Miserable, Theodore wrote in his diary, "...I will try to lead such a life as he would have wished."

Theodore went on long tramps in the woods, crashing through the brush, to outrun his ferocious grief.

He worked even harder at school, "but," he wrote, "I do not care so much for my marks now; what I valued....was *his* pride in them."

Theodore just couldn't stay so sad.
His spirits had to bounce back up.
There was too much for a young man to do.
Besides, he met a young lady.
Young Theodore fell in love with Alice Lee.
After graduation, after he and Elliot got back
from camping in the West, Theodore and Alice were
married on his 22nd birthday, October 27, 1880.

They lived in his family's house. Every
morning, Theodore walked down narrow,
cobblestoned Fifth Avenue to his classes at the
Columbia Law School.

He worked on the book he was writing
about the War of 1812.

He had fun at the opera, skating parties,
sleigh rides, dances, balls, receptions, dinners,
concerts, and teas all dressed up with Alice,
and New York society.

But Theodore wanted more.

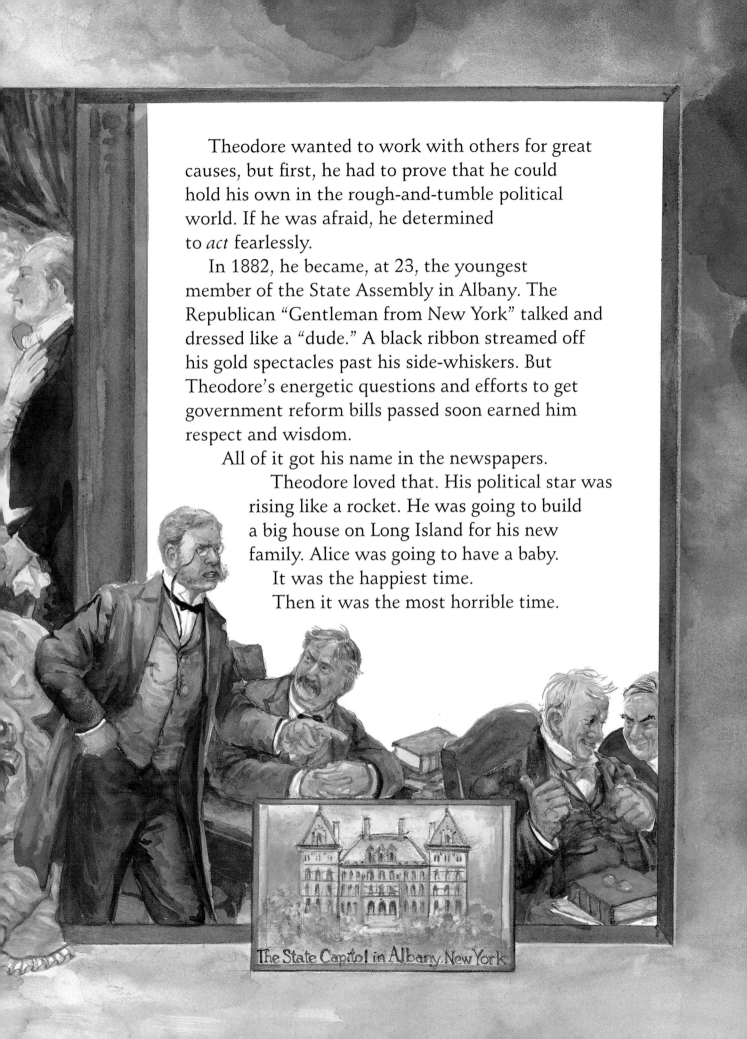

Theodore wanted to work with others for great causes, but first, he had to prove that he could hold his own in the rough-and-tumble political world. If he was afraid, he determined to *act* fearlessly.

In 1882, he became, at 23, the youngest member of the State Assembly in Albany. The Republican "Gentleman from New York" talked and dressed like a "dude." A black ribbon streamed off his gold spectacles past his side-whiskers. But Theodore's energetic questions and efforts to get government reform bills passed soon earned him respect and wisdom.

All of it got his name in the newspapers.

Theodore loved that. His political star was rising like a rocket. He was going to build a big house on Long Island for his new family. Alice was going to have a baby.

It was the happiest time.

Then it was the most horrible time.

The State Capitol in Albany, New York

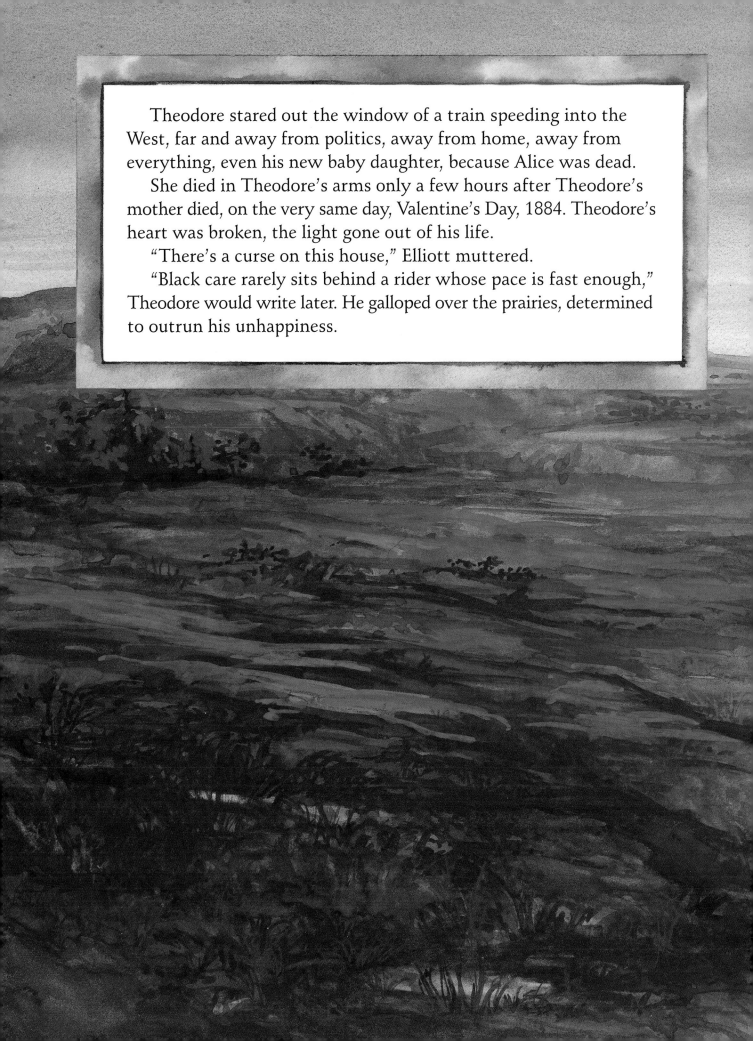

Theodore stared out the window of a train speeding into the West, far and away from politics, away from home, away from everything, even his new baby daughter, because Alice was dead.

She died in Theodore's arms only a few hours after Theodore's mother died, on the very same day, Valentine's Day, 1884. Theodore's heart was broken, the light gone out of his life.

"There's a curse on this house," Elliott muttered.

"Black care rarely sits behind a rider whose pace is fast enough," Theodore would write later. He galloped over the prairies, determined to outrun his unhappiness.

Theodore worked as a cattleman on two ranches in the badlands of the valley of the Little Missouri River.

Occasionally, he went East to see Bamie and his baby, little Alice. He watched his big house being built at Oyster Bay. Once, Bamie, who worried about her lonely brother, made sure Theodore met Edith Carow, their childhood friend. But mostly Theodore worked in the West alongside the cowboys.

ROOSEVELT IN THE DAKOTA
TERRITORY
1884~1886

CANADA

Red River of the North

Elkhorn Ranch

Beaver Creek

Medora
Maltese Cross
Ranch

MONTANA
Territory

Little Missouri River

DAKOTA Territory

Missouri River

The cattle and horses
on Theodore's
two ranches were
branded with
the Elkhorn

or
the Maltese
or a △ Cross

WYOMING
Territory

BLACK
HILLS

0   25   50
miles

De Smet

Sioux Falls

James River

MINNESOTA

IOWA

NEBRASKA

The cowboys laughed at Theodore's glasses—his "storm windows" they called them. They laughed at his dude way of talking. He not only read books every spare moment, he wrote them! But Theodore proved his worth with 16-hours-in-the-saddle days, with his fists, and stubborn grit. He'd eaten dust. He'd grown strong. He'd won his spurs as a Westerner.

And he just couldn't stay so sad.

It was time to go home.

He sailed across the ocean to England. Edith Carow was waiting for him there. They were married in London, December 2, 1886.

Her father gave three-year-old Alice piggyback rides 'round his house, called Sagamore Hill. Over the next ten years, Theodore and Edith had five more children: Theodore Jr. in 1887; Kermit in 1889; Ethel in 1891, "a jolly naughty whacky baby," wrote Theodore; Archibald came in 1894; and Quentin in 1897.

Theodore loved being a boy with all his "bunnies." He led them on romps in the hayloft, in pillow fights in the bedrooms, and on cross-country hikes to picnics and campfires. Sometimes, with the firelight flickering on his spectacles, Theodore moaned and rumbled ghost stories.

The children shrieked with terror and delight.

Theodore called himself a "literary feller." He wrote magazine articles and books about history and the Western life.

He returned to politics in May 1889, when President Harrison appointed him to the U. S. Civil Service Commission. It would be his job for the next six years to make sure government jobs were awarded fairly and done properly. No matter how mad the politicians got, no matter how many times his name was in newspapers all over the country, he'd keep working.

"By Godfrey!" Theodore would exclaim when he got excited. He loved stirring things up.

And that's what he did when he became New York City's police commissioner in 1895. Cloaked in black, hat pulled low, Theodore stalked the city's streets at night.

Was a criminal in the act? Was a policeman snoring when he was supposed to be keeping the peace? Soon the culprit would be looking into eyes narrowed behind their spectacles, and bright white teeth like a row of little tombstones.

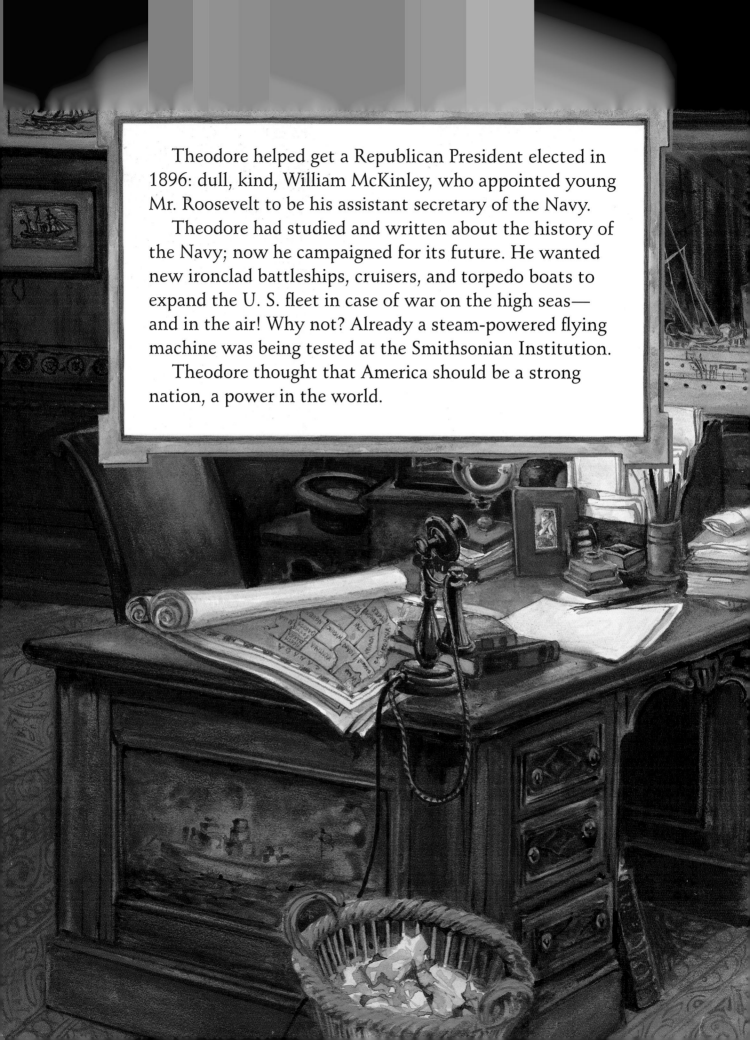

Theodore helped get a Republican President elected in 1896: dull, kind, William McKinley, who appointed young Mr. Roosevelt to be his assistant secretary of the Navy.

Theodore had studied and written about the history of the Navy; now he campaigned for its future. He wanted new ironclad battleships, cruisers, and torpedo boats to expand the U. S. fleet in case of war on the high seas—and in the air! Why not? Already a steam-powered flying machine was being tested at the Smithsonian Institution.

Theodore thought that America should be a strong nation, a power in the world.

WM. McKINLEY

THE WORLD

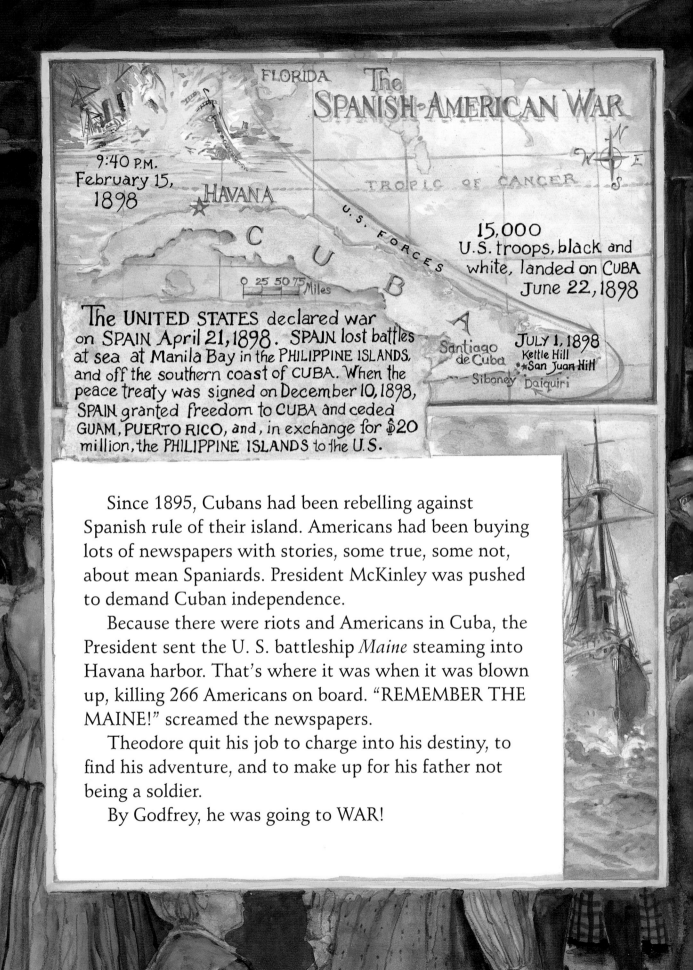

FLORIDA

The SPANISH-AMERICAN WAR

9:40 P.M.
February 15,
1898

HAVANA

TROPIC OF CANCER

U.S. FORCES

C U B A

0 25 50 75 Miles

15,000
U.S. troops, black and
white, landed on CUBA
June 22, 1898

The UNITED STATES declared war on SPAIN April 21, 1898. SPAIN lost battles at sea at Manila Bay in the PHILIPPINE ISLANDS, and off the southern coast of CUBA. When the peace treaty was signed on December 10, 1898, SPAIN granted freedom to CUBA and ceded GUAM, PUERTO RICO, and, in exchange for $20 million, the PHILIPPINE ISLANDS to the U.S.

Santiago
de Cuba

JULY 1, 1898
Kettle Hill
★ ★ San Juan Hill

Siboney Daiquiri

Since 1895, Cubans had been rebelling against Spanish rule of their island. Americans had been buying lots of newspapers with stories, some true, some not, about mean Spaniards. President McKinley was pushed to demand Cuban independence.

Because there were riots and Americans in Cuba, the President sent the U. S. battleship *Maine* steaming into Havana harbor. That's where it was when it was blown up, killing 266 Americans on board. "REMEMBER THE MAINE!" screamed the newspapers.

Theodore quit his job to charge into his destiny, to find his adventure, and to make up for his father not being a soldier.

By Godfrey, he was going to WAR!

About a thousand cowboys, New York policemen, college athletes, actors, society gentlemen, and soldiers of fortune got together to ride in the First U. S. Volunteer Cavalry Regiment. That was its official name, anyway.

Mostly they were known as Colonel Teddy's "Rough Riders."

They charged through gunfire up the steep hills around Santiago de Cuba.

That steamy, bloody July 1, 1898—"the great day of my life," said Theodore—skyrocketed him into legend—and into the next chapter of his life.

The people of New York elected forty-year-old "Colonel Teddy" to be their new governor, November 5, 1898. Theodore worked to preserve New York's natural resources and to make its government and schools run smoothly and fairly. He gave super-patriotic speeches around the country about a strong America's place in the world. He chopped the air with his hands as his high voice carried over parasols and flowered hats, straw hats and derbies. Under them were crowds of people cheering, "We want Teddy!"

The Republicans needed a candidate for Vice President to be on the ticket for President McKinley's re-election in 1900.

Wearing his Rough Rider hat, Theodore strode firmly into the Republican Convention in Philadelphia.

The politicians, wearing McKinley badges on their crumpled seersucker suits, took their cigars out of their mouths to shout "We want Teddy! We want Teddy!"

They nominated him to be the vice presidential candidate, June 21, 1900.

A little over a year later, in September, Theodore was hiking high in the Adirondack mountains when, as in horrible times past, he was called to a death bed. President McKinley, who'd been shot by an assassin, had taken a turn for the worst.

A wagon bouncing and racketing down the dark mountain road carried Theodore to the train to Buffalo, New York.

President McKinley died there early in the morning of the 14th of September, 1901. Sternly, solemnly, 42-year-old Theodore Roosevelt lifted his right hand and took the Oath of Office, the youngest man ever to do so.

In his heart was fierce excitement at becoming the 26th in an unbroken line of Presidents of the United States of America.

THE AUTHOR WISHES TO THANK
Kathleen Young Sheedy, Curator, Sagamore Hill National Historic Site;
Bruce Kaye, Park Ranger, Theodore Roosevelt National Park in Medora, North Dakota;
and Carl Mehler, Senior Map Editor, National Geographic Society, for their assistance.
Please note that place names, such as Rumania, are correct for the time period.

BIBLIOGRAPHY

Lorant, Stefan. *The Life and Times of Theodore Roosevelt*.
New York: Doubleday & Co., Inc., 1959.

McCullough, David. *Mornings on Horseback*.
New York: Simon & Schuster, 1981.

Miller, Nathan. *Theodore Roosevelt, A Life*.
New York: William Morrow and Company, Inc., 1992.

Morris, Sylvia Jukes. *Edith Kermit Roosevelt*.
New York: Coward, McCann & Geoghegan, Inc., 1980.

The Society is supported through membership dues
and income from the sale of its educational products.
Call 1-800-NGS-LINE for more information.
Visit our website at www.nationalgeographic.com.

Library of Congress Cataloging-in-Publication Data

Harness, Cheryl.
Young Teddy Roosevelt / by Cheryl Harness.
p. cm.
Summary: Briefly traces the life of Theodore Roosevelt,
from his privileged childhood through the personal tragedies
he endured to his swearing in as the twenty-sixth president of the United States.
ISBN 0-7922-7094-0
1. Roosevelt, Theodore, 1858-1919—Juvenile literature.
2. Roosevelt, Theodore, 1858-1919—Childhood and youth—Juvenile literature.
3. Presidents—United States—Biography—Juvenile literature.
[1. Roosevelt, Theodore, 1858-1919. 2. Presidents.]
I. Title.
E757.H33 1998
973.91'1'092   [B]—DC21   97-24061   CIP

Printed in Hong Kong

704·j